DC DAYS

Poems

Neal Stayton Pratt

Copyright © 2020 by Neal Pratt. All rights reserved.
ISBN 978-1-73436-610-5

Neal Pratt Publishing
Printed in the United States of America

Cover Art by Dima Drjuchin
Design & Layout by Owen Pratt

Also by Neal Stayton Pratt

Sights & Recollections

This Page Intentionally Left Blank

Meaning of Numbers

The Awful Waiting

Everything Looks Prettier Under Candlelight

It's Been a Long Ugly Winter

You Can't Progress without a Few Calluses

First Day of Spring

Before You Know Your Fate

for Shelly

POEMS

Beat Hotel	09	Copy Paper	43
88 Bleeker Street	10	Rusmey Aquatic Center	44
Someplace Sunny	11	Seattle Part I	45
Fragmented Thoughts	12	Seattle Part II	46
The Absinthe House	13	A Walk in the Sun	47
Salinger (notes)	14	Give Me a Thought	49
Washington DC Part I	15	Notebook Love	50
Washington DC Part II	16	War	51
Washington DC Part III	17	Greyhound Bound	52
Birthday	18	Thursday Afternoon (Bronchitis)	53
January 4th, Day of Loss	19	Thursday (2 weeks later)	54
Day of Remembrance	20	Friday November 18th	55
Shoes	21	Back to…	56
White Roses	22	Inauguration	57
Franco Cesana	23	Women's March on Washington	58
Venting	24	4th Street Heat	59
Jefferson Memorial	25	Waiting to See	61
Ellis Island Haikus	26	A Brief Snow Shower at 2:45p.m.	62
Train Song	27	Fire on the 9th Floor	63
Day of Meditation #1	28	Graveyards	64
Day of Meditation #2	29	Habits	65
Eight Ball Aesthetics	30	Gettysburg Part I	66
Day of Infestation	31	Wine & Thought	67
Cold Rains in the District	32	Gettysburg Part II	68
Test	33	Captain	69
Wine Pickers	34	DC Fair	70
Day in February of a Certain Year	35	Kingman Island	71
DC Day #...	36	R.F.K.	72
Alley Activity	37	Bike Ride	73
Jonathan Riley	38	Flag Post	75
Pond Poem #1	39	Zombies	76
Pond Poem #2	40	DCFD	77
Willow Words	41	Congressional Cemetery	78
Testimonies	42		

DC DAYS

Poems

Beat Hotel

poets crouched in cozy corners

reading mad rants that battle

the traffic noises seeping in

from the cracks in the rotting caulk

surrounding the melting stained-glass

windowpane that purifies the light.

"artists only!" she cried.

aspirations gained through hallucination,

they double down on life.

88 Bleeker Street

The rumble of the subway below
Shakes my thoughts loose from the crevices,
And I watch them fall to the floor.

I pick them up gently,
Rearranging them like furniture on polished hardwood,
As they fall to the page.

The sounds are sweet lullabies
That soothe my anxious soul-
An orchestra of ringing.

Squeaking roars overtake grinding beeps
Awaking platform pedestrians
And the buried on Bowery.

Growling engines give to
Squeaking brakes that echo to
The rumble of the subway below.

SOMEPLACE SUNNY

I need someplace sunny, honey,

I've got the money,

let's get away for a while.

Some day I'll go insane

so you can drop my name.

My ashes scattered to the ground,

it took some energy,

but finally she found me

sitting alone on a train.

FRAGMENTED THOUGHTS

The strumming goes on into the night
tickling the trees swaying to the beat,

into the night where so many
travel through alleys and parkways,

skipping stones in abandoned ponds;
fingers are blistered from the friction,

the vibration still plows through these bones
where words are eternal,

although I'm just passing through.
I can tell through lover's eyes

that she is tired of the blues.
Fragmented thoughts explode onto the pages,

where cramped hands tirelessly try to keep up
with the stenographer in my mind.

THE ABSINTHE HOUSE

milky green minds

hang under the spotlight

that throws halos

violent in color

violet in hue

SALINGER (NOTES)

Poker table odds
swinging in your favor,

slight rebellion off Madison.
A shadow in the story

when we used to write letters,
back before the war.

Serving in the Army
Normandy, France

Utah Beach
1944

"A Perfect Day For Banana Fish"
after a perfectly awful war.

A shooting star that turned the light off
after the spotlight of terror witnessed at large.

A lady's man gifted with the art of poetry,
but the people don't know what you've been through.

The bodies stacked,
the walking on the beach,

the David Copperfield crap,
a scratchy needle on a phonograph.

WASHINGTON DC PART I

The humming never really ends
on 19th Street Northeast, Washington, DC.

They strum their hum
all night long,

and buzz through the day,
drowning out the sun.

My ears grow deaf to the sirens
and lights that creep through crevices

of the drapes and light up
my sleeping ceiling.

WASHINGTON DC PART II

The streetlights signal
to only the wind

as it whips through
the abandoned city streets.

The grey skies are replaced
by glowing holiday lights

that seem to bring
a little warmth to the bitter cold.

WASHINGTON DC PART III

They leave in droves, exiting the city
as the folders sit dormant on the desks.

Lights are strung up haphazardly,
outlining the door and window frames

that show the holiday parties in full swing.
There should be snow-covered streets by now,

but the winter is on strike and may never return.
The homeless fight for the subway vents

that shoot warmth up from down below,
just in case the weeks turn frigid in the future.

A bustling city that feels empty
with the abundance of vacant parking spaces,

lonely crying in the night,
causing the streetlights to flicker

on
off
on.

BIRTHDAY

So here it is,
another marker on the timeline.

Each year they get less important,
dream sleepy Saturday

as the weather changes
to reflect the fact that leaves have fallen.

Manual labor sweating,
dragging the rake across the debris.

The dust of dead concrete
come flying in the alley.

JANUARY 4TH, DAY OF LOSS

It came so suddenly
and left just as quickly,
but the images will always remain.

Masses that spread
shaking with pain
lying in the snow waiting to die.

Decisions and choices,
which ones are right?
i needed you here, but that is selfish.

Borrowed blanket
pacing the tile
as if you knew your fate.

Eyes closed and breathing slow
until your last was taken,
and I was crushed.

We attempt to pick up the pieces
of the shattered life that appears
behind every corner.

Blue velvet pouch
wrapped double with a bow,
that holds the package secure,

hiding in the box
with the beautiful red oak stain
with a brass plaque in loving memory of you.

DAY OF REMEMBRANCE

I'll put you up on my shelf
just above my record collection,

in front of the Archers of Loaf pennant,
on top of my Magnet magazines,

just above the opening aspiration,
and leave you staring at the picture

of Mingur Yongey Rinpoche
while my speakers sound the silvery

streets of Avery Island
because that's where I'd want to be,
if I had nowhere to go.

SHOES

Saved for their musty scent

no skin

no teeth

just that leathery gleam

that were piled high

beneath the white

puffy ash

that billows in the dark.

WHITE ROSES

Brave soldiers

executed for beliefs

wooden bridges to Warsaw

mark their path

of resistance

and existence.

FRANCO CESANA

Late September in 1931

life seemed so simple,

life seemed so fun

until the law came down

and sent you away.

Though your father died,

you kept by your mother's side,

and joined the justice at only 12.

Scouting a mission,

you were shot in the mountains.

Your body returned

on your 13th birthday,

and you were the youngest

partisan to die for the cause.

VENTING

And as long as i'm getting things off my chest,

I never said that you were the best

and you're just a number like we all are

forever floating to meet in the sun.

And as I look out

over the window spout

I see you as you were when you were younger

with your dreams talking to the trees.

Your perfume smells good

hanging in the breeze

that blows through your sunset hair that floats over me.

Why can't you see that I'm lonely and need a companion?

She walks toward me, stalking,

my heart races, innocently

until we see we are changing into ourselves.

We shed our skins, our former selves,

and lift our souls up to the sun.

JEFFERSON MEMORIAL

The cherry blossoms beckon the tourists,
illuminating the path with pinks and

whites that patiently pose for snapping cameras
until you fall to the ground, staining the concrete

with your hues that run off to the basin
where the swans dance in the dye.

The color guard march rigid legs
as Jefferson judges from the back.

Board members are thanked with brass plaques
bearing achievements of the year.

A wreath is saluted and presented to you
in honor of your 271st birthday

as the band strikes up its ceremonial song,
and sends us into a salutation frenzy.

ELLIS ISLAND HAIKUS

history abounds
within the overgrown grass
sick, poor, and wretched

make it a museum
hang the photos of the babes
and polio deaths

strip down to your skin
as you climb the stair case
saluting the flag

interviews abound
as the conveyor belt moves
human power plant

horses tower up
and shadow wings spread out
american now

we'll patch you up right
wash and scrub your skin clean
and ship you back home

the white tile screams
echo against the ceiling
deathly harmonies

scarlet fever hits
the ones too young to know
kids wrapped in linen

medicine testing
on the unfortunate ones
graphing your progress

immigrant migration
travelling west to escape
ellis island

TRAIN SONG

Thundering steel on steel
hurling itself down the track
as if straight through my brain.

The steady beats send my limbs
moving to the repetitive vibration,
and jolts my heart back to life.

The rumbling drowns out the traffic
that race home at mid-day,
leaving the sonic echo vibrating below.

The last car passes in time
taking with it the rattling of the boxcar
that sends the fading sounds of a train into the distance.

DAY OF MEDITATION #1

I can focus on the constant roar
of city noises,

and use them as pillars
that mercilessly hold up my spirituality.

Dodging raindrops in the park,
but bare legs

and lined pages
don't balk at the thought.

Another train catches me off guard
with the sounding of the horn,

57 cars and counting until finally
the sounds dissipate in the distance.

My bench companion provides
adequate shelter

with its full umbrella canopy, tiny sounds of breaking glass
echo from the pavement.

DAY OF MEDITATION #2

The stale metallic aroma
burns my nostrils

and is broken only by the breeze
from the oncoming train.

We move ourselves toward
the opening doors

like cattle herding themselves home
and searching for an empty seat.

Morning time is standing time,
maybe a seat to yourself

in the afternoon, or maybe a car
sitting alone and staring at the silence.

Meditate to the thunk-thunk of the wheels
grinding on the track as my thoughts and emotions

fill the empty seats, and cram themselves into the aisle
like rush hour commuter traffic.

Eight Ball Aesthetics

When one sits,
one must produce something special to the audience

in the form of clouds.
Hard rhythm playing to a sweaty crowd.

Eight ball aesthetics
with arrows in the road.

See his reflection in the mirror
his future is sold now.

Rosemary prayers
do nothing to your soul.

Fake it 'till you forget it
'till you have more control.

What would you say to you and me?

Day of Infestation

The mice have become brave,
testing the distance limits,
three, four, maybe more.

Prancing feet echoes in the dark corners,
scurrying along the baseboards,
three, four, maybe more.

The babies are braver than most,
showing their faces in broad daylight,
three, four, maybe more.

Dark shadows trick my eyes,
to where I question sanity,
three, four, maybe more.

COLD RAINS IN THE DISTRICT

Steady rains fall bravely,
sacrificing themselves
to the pavement below.

splat
        splat
                splat

Gathering into rippled puddles that sidetracks
the sidewalk walker balancing on the curb,
mangled from the tree roots.

Rivers flow downhill,
gaining speed on 19th Street, and
washing the crime down two blocks.

A lake engulfs us all,
leaving our chilled bodies
clinging to the crests.

TEST

this is a test,

a test to see if the pen was empty and
dried up like my thoughts lately.

an abandoned stream

that no longer has the strength
to shape the stones lying dormant.

dammed up,

causing the fish to vacate
and search for food elsewhere.

too many distortions

and not enough focus on the pillars
to overcome the obstacles.

WINE PICKERS

century
old
recipes
developed
by
backs
that
break
aloft
the hills
of
Burgundy

TEST

this is a test,

a test to see if the pen was empty and
dried up like my thoughts lately.

an abandoned stream

that no longer has the strength
to shape the stones lying dormant.

dammed up,

causing the fish to vacate
and search for food elsewhere.

too many distortions

and not enough focus on the pillars
to overcome the obstacles.

WINE PICKERS

century
old
recipes
developed
by
backs
that
break
aloft
the hills
of
Burgundy

A Day in February of a Certain Year

I've been all over this city today:

up 16th Street to the northwest,

back to the northeast,

and the southwest,

out to the train,

through the southeast.

Bitter winds chill my shiny bones

as I walk faster to counter

the numbness growing from my cheeks.

Slowly I start to stumble

and stagger for balance

with a frozen equilibrium.

Curled up in the corner,

staying current with events

as the zombies hurdle my thin shoes.

DC Day #...(for J.T.)

after a little e.e. and tate
i retreat to a tea shop

where i am disappointed with the selections,
but enlightened by the muse.

everyday events

playedoutinwords

for

      you

           to

                  read.

"Mr. youse needen't be so spry,"
for your white donkey

has drank himself in a ha-ha
before stepping up to the podium

and declaring that all things are round,
tipping his hat to the three ghosts

singing backup harmonies
that could melt the angels' wings.

"we could be here all night,"
i heard someone whisper.

ALLEY ACTIVITY

I could probably set my watch to it,
or at least align the stars

to the perfectly timed trips
the old man makes through the alley.

His shuffle is constant
no matter what the weather.

More reliable than the postal service,
always the nod or occasional passing greeting

as we make eye contact
and ponder how it got this bad.

To the store and back again
with the same shuffle,

thrice daily to replenish
his quench for freedom.

Jonathan Riley

Bodies stacked between the windows
searching for seeps of air and
dodging bodies that keep floating past.

The cool air summons you
as you fight the heat
that singes your arm hair.

One last decision and a leap to give your
lungs one more chance to breathe
while your heartbeat takes control.

arms flapping

legs flailing

spinning out of control

until the shadows block the sun and
leave your body mangled on sidewalk
cracks that called you home.

POND POEM #1

Park sounds abound
with the occasional jet engine

that rumbles past behind
the reflecting pool drained for repairs.

The chirps provide the beat
as the sirens blare over the background.

An occasional baby cry
or page turn peaks my ears

while my eyes are distracted
by the bustling of the park.

Fountains bubbling up
exciting the seagulls

as the tourists toss purchased squares
to the ducks wading in the pond.

I spot a new green dress
with a determined walk

from across the pond,
but lost her to the willows

and the blue shorts
lounging to my right.

POND POEM #2

Three unicyclists just rode right past
all dressed in their Sunday best.

(although it's a Monday)

Legs turning the wheels in the
off beat rhythm as they pass the pond.

The ducks can't decide if they are with
the Mormons or the circus set up stakes.

The crowd takes notice of the novel act
pausing their tour for a brief minute

before continuing their steady
gait hoping to catch a glimpse

of the cherry blossoms that welcome
with open petals pink

before the last one is carried to newly
cut grass by a breeze across the basin.

WILLOW WORDS

Air cools the blood
that has escaped my veins

when the pedal split my sweaty skin.
Its crimson glow spreads out like a city

map and flows like the Potomac
that gently carries paddle boarders down stream.

The willows shade and protect me
from the jet engine roars that

keep rhythm for the leaves
playing their tambourines in the wind.

Ants drink up the salty sensation
leaving them inebriated in mediocrity

with a burning desire to open their umbrellas
and be blown away with the

wind onto another colony where they will
speculate and judge their neighbors,

forming governments at local levels
that get overthrown at will,

and tell all the old stories of how,
long ago they drank the red river that

planted the future in their heads
strengthening their exoskeleton.

TESTIMONIES (FOR E.E.)

one page testimonies
that's all they are supposed to be

no abstract thought
or terrible lists

but the dismantling of my heart
reassembled delicately onto these

perfectly spaced thirty one lined pages
that mock me with their emptiness.

line
by
line

the words spill out like my cut skin
with no rhyme

and certainly no
REAS

ON
rUlEsArEmAdEtObEbRoKeN,

but I have my doubts.

Copy Paper

Without my little book
I resort to copy paper

that still bears the errors
tossed in a bin.

I give it new life
with my hot pen

that dances wildly
across each line

with barely legible writing
and even harder to find meaning.

RUSMEY AQUATIC CENTER

It's been a dismal summer
with little productivity.

I gather from the few filled pages
as I flip back to remember what I wrote.

Sitting poolside the voices echo
against the roof and bounce

through the empty air,
looming just above our heads.

The life guard catches up on sleep
while little feet splash a rhythm all their own.

All indoor pools smell the same with the
stale humidity mixed with the chlorine

leaving a damp potency in the nostrils.
The ripples in the water provide a

hypnotic reflection of the far windows that
put me in a trance imagining

I was anywhere but here.

SEATTLE PART I

Crazy thoughts hang over
the cool skies with

the moon glowing
burnt orange, looming

over the Seattle skies.
"Crash Shop" sign hangs

proudly, lighting the
yellowed-bricked wall

of the auto shop.
The tall garage is

a dead give away,
1950 drama seeps

from the unlit neon
sign that reads,

"Open Office."

SEATTLE PART II

I watch the plane
play chicken with the moon

and glide effortlessly
across the sky,

hovering above the proud office
lights, giving protection

in the dark hours,
on the border of chaos

and remembering
from across the room.

A Walk in the Sun

I love the sun as it warms
my face from the chill in the air.

A week before thanksgiving,
and the rich blue sky cools my lungs.

I sit in the car observing,
watching the people walk past

astonished at the ground covered
when I find them again.

I stare off, dreaming
blindly at the flag

proudly protesting
the discussion of the day.

Cars filter in for the pickups
like a taxi line at Union Station

that wraps all the way to H Street.
I've never seen anyone,

from empty offices
that loom above the street

not once,

not a soul

on ten floors and a block wide.
Personal decorations are seen

as if abandoned in such a rush
like the purses left hanging

on the back of the chairs
when the buildings fell.

I climb out of my trance
and take a deep breath

of the chilled air and go back
to critiquing sloppy parking jobs.

GIVE ME A THOUGHT

Give me a thought

just one little thought

to make this barricade fall.

Give me a chance

just one little chance

to make all my dreams come true.

NOTEBOOK LOVE

Pretty black ribbon
laying gracefully on the chaise.

I manipulate your shadows
with twists of fingers.

I knot and bow you
wrapped like a package topping.

Once you were a snake
and devoured the crumbs,

once you were a fish
and swam up stream to spawn,

but your true talent
is in keeping progress

as progress creeps by
at a snail's pace in July.

You mock my efforts
hiding between black lines

that guide me to the end
and force me to turn the page.

WAR

the
        next
                war
                        will
                                be
between

                        the
                ones
        and
zeros.

GREYHOUND BOUND

Greyhound bound

to New York City.

Crammed in my seat

I sleep when I can.

The sun parts the clouds

and wakes me from my

dreary-eyed haze.

Country songs carry on

in my brain for a week straight.

The traffic lulls at the tolls,

but the momentum is on my side.

The green trees blur

as the bus speeds up the highway

as the blue skies show us all the way.

THURSDAY AFTERNOON (BRONCHITIS)

I emerge from my slumber

disheveled and disorientated-

stumble to the closet with aching chest

to retrieve my little book.

Exhausting energy just to write

nonsense down as it comes

slowly like the tide,

and before you know it

the water is at your ankles

with toes buried in the wet sand.

Stopping to rest and conserve

motion for when I'll truly need them-

later today, perhaps

when the pain eases its reins,

and lets me think in solitude once again.

THURSDAY (2 WEEKS LATER)

The golden voice left us to listen

to the groveling from the street.

Words were pure poetry

that rang true within our sheets,

timeless in wisdom

too free to be told

with a window to the angles

and a key to your soul.

NOVEMBER 18TH, FRIDAY

The sirens won't cease
as the leaves twirl

downward and parade proudly
displaying their fall hues. The blues

are playing and fits the mood
between the conversation

and squeals that scream
into the distance,

endlessly echoing through
the cloudless blue wonder.

BACK TO...

back to the early morning wake ups

back to the morning making tea

back to the laundry piles

back to the organization

back to picking up after the girls

back to early morning glow of the sun

that shines against the red-bricked

apartment complex

and slaps my eyes awake

back to the blocks that prevent

the flow to the page

back to the doubt that looms overhead

back to the nerves that build from the pressure

back to the plans and arrangements

back to the shiny razors that kiss my cheeks clean

and bring pores to life

hungry for fresh air

INAUGURATION

The district streets are empty
most stay inside-
the faces you do see are sullen and lost.

Only tourists and protesters are out,
and gather under the monitors
to witness the sacred oath of destruction.

Crowds are sparse in comparison
to the protesters that stand up
for democracy through peaceful resistance.

Tangible freedom not just national jargon
spewed onto battlefields
motivating troops to torch.

Visiting vandals insert destruction
and mayhem with shattered glass
and 95 arrests.

January day looms,
rain begins falling as he speaks
as if god himself were appalled.

Wind blows and parking abounds
as I drive around the abandoned town
with a sad emptiness in my heart.

Women's March on Washington

What a difference a day
and a message makes.

Turnout is staggering to imagine-
every square foot filled with citizens

from all over the country
holding signs:

some funny
some sad

all creative
all expressions of love

one love and UNITY.
Millions as one

throughout the world
joining in dissent.

Wake up white men;
you've upset the ladies.

4TH STREET HEAT

"This heat is almost unbearable"
I explained to myself.

I have sold my shirt to my sweat
that is attacking every pore.

We prayed for a warm sunlight
all through winter

digging out our cars,
buried in the drifts.

The warmth has come and gone
like a one night stand

and left the heat in its place
as a reminder of the night before.

The fans are useless
pushing the hot air closer to my body.

I laugh at its swivel-headed brilliance,
praying for the poor

bastards who have to sleep here.
It must be cooler outside

than in this room,
thirty feet above the pedestrians

who count the sweat beads
that drip to the pavement,

from their foreheads,
slowly walking home.

The fresh collared shirts
are a darker hue

from the quickened pace
and heavy load.

Waiting to See

always waiting
always waiting to see
what happens next

always watching
always watching to see
what happens next

a quiet observer from the sidelines

patient
unsure
timid
scared

headlights don't bend around corners

nervous
free
exciting
joy

always waiting
always waiting to see
what happens next

A Brief Snow Shower at 2:45pm

Out from the clearing
a brief snow shower,

a lone blizzard
floating over the homes,

down 21st Street
through the soccer fields

to play a quick match.
As soon as it came

it left just as fast,
leaving the sunbeams in its trail

that glisten the dead leaves
still clinging to the spiny

branches of winter,
brittle to the touch.

FIRE ON THE 9TH FLOOR

The ninety bodies
came falling
from the sky.

The ones that were left
were charred and
hanging from a rope

up on the 9th floor
with 300 packed in tight
to increase production.

Now we recognize them
by their stockings that are pulled tight
and fray from the fire.

The lower east side cries tonight,
still seven that can't be identified
under the wool blankets.

Finally laid to rest
under protest of 100 thousand
who march onto Brooklyn with rage.

Exits doors were blocked
to prevent lost cloth inventory,
but not as guilty as the verdict

and its all the same to you.
Without regulations
people cut corners that costs lives.

GRAVEYARDS

Graveyards along the rural routes
always leave me sad.

Such a lonely place to spend eternity,
where cars go flying past, hourly.

Looking for familiar names
as I speed past and capture

"Forrester" and "Christianson"
with my head slightly twisted

down and to the right,
focusing for a second

and then letting it go by.
Three miles from the memorial to

Stonewall Jackson,
driving home in the rain

that has pounded and drizzled
for the past three hours.

I pass the route, pointing the way
steady gas forward

the girls and I venture on,
striving for home.

HABITS

Repetitions and habits are my thing,
but my habits ruin the plan of the day.

Always something to do
and never enough time

to do the fun things.
Wasted time in a blur of minutes,

as the grains rapidly
fall to the base of the curved glass.

I pick it up and rotate the sands
until the weight of the grains

finds the path of gravity,
starting my clock over.

Phoenix from the ashes
wondering how many

more cycles can I take
until enlightenment.

GETTYSBURG PART I

A little black book
filled with thoughts and dreams

writing what I see
but it isn't all that it seems.

Aural bombardment rings my ears
breaking my balanced stagger.

Smoke makes hazy silhouettes
that eerily move against the contrast

running scared through skinny trees,
tasting bark blown into the mouths.

Rebel yell from old grey beard
exciting troops begging for quick death.

WINE & THOUGHT

Wine and thought
smoke and dreams.

Visual appearance
isn't what it seems.

Shadows and doors
from outside porch.

Religious symbols
searching to find

a meaning of it all
so lost within the time.

Should be a century earlier
writing rhymes on banks of the Seine.

GETTYSBURG PART II

Beliefs collide
sending shrapnel
through limbs.

Musket oak to musket oak
combat force explodes
with clouds of confusion.

The midday sky
black from the blaze
perfumes the rotting corpses

that lie still
from yesterdays' conquests
where more than egos die.

CAPTAIN

Century old image repeated
like his lists that hang long

like his grey madman beard,
growing whiter with the grief.

On and
on and on

the lilacs
the lilacs.

The lilac bush that grows
just over the windowpane

and leaves the warm aroma
in your nostrils as your face

hits the spring morning.
A single tear falls to the deck

and will evaporate just as quickly
in the southern morning heat

as we march five abreast
across the Mason-Dixon line.

DC Fair

All that's left of the DC fair
is just a fence line protecting air

nestled just underneath the metro line
inviting the neighborhood to the party.

Flashing lights and a carousel
organ tunes and a Ferris Wheel

distorted voices carry across the tent,
spent $12 and nothing to show for it.

Clash of the cultures, but all
are enjoying the scene.

Spin so fast, you'll want to scream,
Capitol dome towers over the neighborhood

trees as our carriage climbs,
searching for the only breeze in DC.

Kingman Island

On cool days
before the heat
brings mosquitos.

I travel East
across the lot
to Kingman Island.

Follow your feet
around the trail
and back again.

Wooden piers
creak with weight
as we walk past

empty bottles linger
on the shoreline
exposing our lazy habits.

The worn path
shows you the way
over muddy marshes.

A quick break
back to nature
for a few breaths

and back again
across the lot
from Kingman Island.

R.F.K.

The giant structure stands
despite its defeat
from the elements and time.

A shell of past existence
as the pillars struggle
under the weight of the decades.

The once new paint
now sheds its leper skin,
and is blown into the Anacostia breeze.

A single slab of marble
has met its fate in the overgrown grass,
and splits its spirit from the fall.

Vast parking lots expand outwards
and merge along the riverbanks
that wind down to the Navy Yard.

Explosions of color stain the asphalt
in a vibrant palette of pinks,
yellows, reds, and blues,

waiting to be washed away
by the rearing rainstorm
that looms over R.F.K.

BIKE RIDE

From neighborhoods
where tourists don't venture
to the Capitol and down the hill,

past the Hart building
where Comey testified yesterday
right on Pennsylvania Avenue.

Stick a finger out as I
breeze by Trumpf hotel
stuck on 15th street (in the shade).

Motorcade passes: 22 vehicles total,
blue red flashing hot
sending echo past, into the compound.

Put the pedals into motion
past the Reflecting
Pool standing motionless

for the ducks to admire themselves.
Pause at Lincoln and
savor the sound of the breeze,

over to Arlington counting crosses
and on to Rosslyn
where the buildings become vertical.

Crossing the Key bridge,
views abound down river
saluting the tune stuck in my head,

through Georgetown,
cooling my tires
in the fountain spray

and leave a trail swerving
through the pedestrians
passing Watergate. (I think it's comical

that time passes yet we can't seem
to learn from the past).
the choir hits my ears as I ride under the

Kennedy Center that shades my
ambitions for a few revolutions
onward to M.L.K and F.D.R.

Passing the Jefferson and the overlooked
George Mason statue that lounges
in shadows of Jefferson's dome,

trying to keep up as I mingle with
the cyclists around Haynes point
where the river winds

blow planes in the air.
Every minute counting cranes in
the southwest that linger over Captain

White's welcome sign sneaking past the
hill on the south east where libraries
provide stoops to the homeless,

and across on North Carolina
back to the Northeast side of town
where tourists don't venture.

FLAG POST

The orange flag hangs
lazily drooped,
ever so often

raising itself to flap
and linger
in the breeze,

waving to the speeding
cars that race
past the stop sign,

folding over itself
and back again
restless like a child.

The proud shield
displays old
glory of past years.

Orange fabric flapping's
catch my
eye and distracts

the words from
flowing fast
and slows to a drip…

ZOMBIES

Open mouthed and confused,

staggering along the median

like a novice on a beam.

Foot dragging behind

as if it has better ideas for the day.

Dodging traffic

with two different shoes

and a cigarette lip glued

from the dry bond.

Successful scramble to sit in the shade

and start the day by being forgotten.

DCFD

The screaming sirens persist,

sounds bouncing straight

to the stair stoops echoing off E Street,

shaking trees

with high-pitched whines,

building for blocks sounding their shouts,

louder stronger,

piercing pain,

red flashing horn blaring and then gone,

succumbed to distance.

An echo of energy

fading up 21st street.

Four sets of sirens come

and pass.

Somewhere

someone

has more pain than my fragile ears.

Congressional Cemetery

Headstones and hounds abound around
the grounds where the blades

get early morning trims.
Markers stained black with time dripping

down facades smearing names and dates
forgotten to generations.

Fences spread ivy sprouts that patiently
await the hungry goats that pick silver

chain-link clean with insatiable appetites.
Movie night and wine in tombs

next to congressman and assassins alike
who listen intently to the twilight gossip.

Dead don't disturb dogs
that roam with cling clang collars,

sounding from steady gaits
marking the monuments.

www.ingramcontent.com/pod-product-compliance
Lightning Source LLC
Chambersburg PA
CBHW051713040426
42446CB00008B/864